SUPER SANDCASTLE™

It's the Alphabet!

# It's G!

Katherine Hengel

Consulting Editor, Diane Craig, M.A./Reading Specialist

Published by ABDO Publishing Company, 8000 West 78th Street, Edina,
Minnesota 55439. Copyright © 2010 by Abdo Consulting Group, Inc.
International copyrights reserved in all countries. No part of this book may be
reproduced in any form without written permission from the publisher. Super
SandCastle™ is a trademark and logo of ABDO Publishing Company.

Printed in the United States.

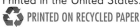 PRINTED ON RECYCLED PAPER

Editor: Liz Salzmann
Content Developer: Nancy Tuminelly
Cover and Interior Design and Production: Kelly Doudna, Mighty Media
Photo Credits: AbleStock, iStockphoto (Jani Bryson), Photodisc, Shutterstock

**Library of Congress Cataloging-in-Publication Data**
Hengel, Katherine.
  It's G! / Katherine Hengel.
    p. cm. -- (It's the alphabet!)
  ISBN 978-1-60453-594-5
  1.  English language--Alphabet--Juvenile literature. 2.  Alphabet books--Juvenile
literature.  I. Title.
  PE1155.H465 2010
  421'.1--dc22

  〈E〉
                        2009020954

Super SandCastle™ books are created by a team of professional educators,
reading specialists, and content developers around five essential components—
phonemic awareness, phonics, vocabulary, text comprehension, and fluency—to
assist young readers as they develop reading skills and strategies and increase
their general knowledge. All books are written, reviewed, and leveled for guided
reading, early reading intervention, and Accelerated Reader® programs for use
in shared, guided, and independent reading and writing activities to support a
balanced approach to literacy instruction.

JEASY
ITS

## About SUPER SANDCASTLE™

**Bigger Books for Emerging Readers
Grades K–4**

Created for library, classroom, and at-home use,
Super SandCastle™ books support and engage
young readers as they develop and build literacy
skills and will increase their general knowledge
about the world around them. Super SandCastle™
books are an extension of SandCastle™, the
leading preK–3 imprint for emerging and beginning
readers. Super SandCastle™ features a larger trim
size for more reading fun.

**Let Us Know**
Super SandCastle™ would like to hear your stories
about reading this book. What was your favorite
page? Was there something hard that you needed
help with? Share the ups and downs of learning to
read. We want to hear from you! Send us an e-mail.

sandcastle@abdopublishing.com

Contact us for a complete list of SandCastle™, Super SandCastle™, and other nonfiction and fiction titles from ABDO Publishing Company.

www.abdopublishing.com • 8000 West 78th Street
Edina, MN 55439 • 800-800-1312 • 952-831-1632 fax

Aa Bb Cc Dd Ee
Ff Gg Hh Ii Jj Kk
Ll Mm Nn Oo Pp
Qq Rr Ss Tt Uu Vv
Ww Xx Yy Zz

# The Letter

# G g

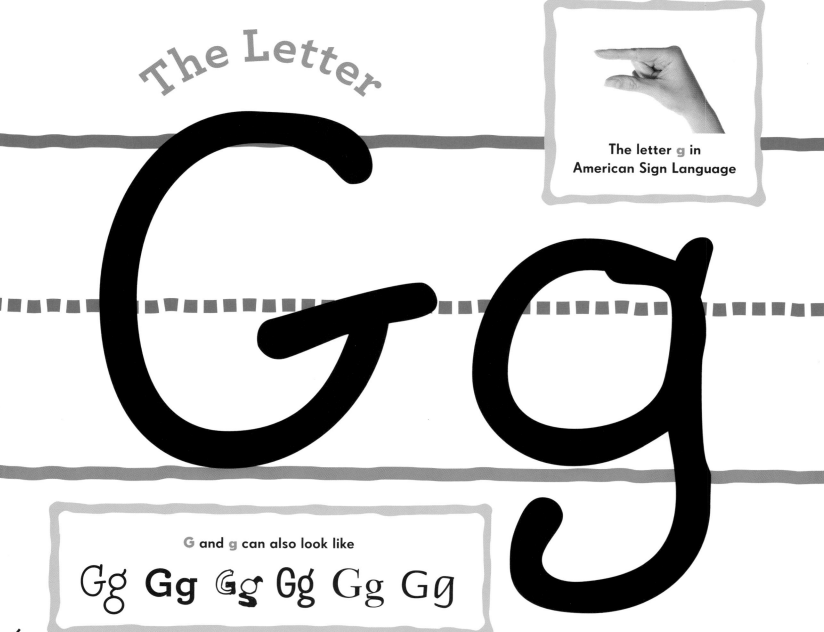

The letter g in
American Sign Language

G and g can also look like

Gg **Gg** Gg Gg Gg Gg

4

The letter g is a consonant.

It is the 7th letter of the alphabet.

hard g as in **goose**

**tiger**

**goose**

**pig**

6

# garden

The pig, the goose, and the tiger play tag in the garden.

soft g as in **g**iant

**pigeon**

**cage**

Paige

No words end with soft g.

Paige keeps her giant pigeon in a huge cage.

9

dge as in ba**dge**

ba**dge**

partri**dge**

A partridge
with a badge
stands on a hedge.

he**dge**

10

ng as in ki**ng**

king

duckling

The king sings a
song while walking
his young duckling.

☞ gh as in night

knight

flashlight

At night, Dwight uses eight flashlights to read about knights.

gn as in **gn**ome

gnome

sign

gnu

The gnome
holds a sign
and rides a gnu.

Gina Kangaroo goes outside to play a game of tag.

She greets eight great pals by the giant green flag.

Gina tags Grace Tiger
by the garden gnome.

She giggles and is glad
she didn't stay home!

Grace tags George Giraffe
who can't get Gavin Stag.

"Gee!" gasps George.
"That stag is good at tag!"

George tags Gina and dodges behind a hedge.

But it's hard for such a giant to hide and gain an edge!

Gina gets excited
and figures she can win.

She gathers all her strength
and grins a huge grin.

Then with one mighty leap,
Gina glides through the air.

She tags George before
he even grasps that she's there!

21

Which words have the
same **g** sound as **go**?

sign

tiger

pig

goose

duckling

flag

stag

cage

# Glossary

**badge** (p. 10) – a small sign or symbol worn to show someone's job or rank.

**dodge** (p. 18) – to suddenly move out of the way of something.

**gasp** (p. 17) – to say something while you are out of breath.

**glide** (p. 20) – to move in a slow and easy manner.

**gnome** (pp. 13, 16) – a character from many folk legends that looks like a short old man.

**gnu** (p. 13) – a large African antelope with a head like an ox and curved horns.

**grasp** (p. 20) – to realize or understand.

**hedge** (pp. 10, 18) – a fence or wall made by planting shrubs or small trees very close together.

To promote letter recognition, letters are highlighted instead of glossary words in this series. The page numbers above indicate where the glossary words can be found.

## More Words with G

Find the **g** in the beginning, middle, or end of each word.

| | | | | |
|---|---|---|---|---|
| again | feeling | gift | grow | hog |
| begin | fight | girl | guard | large |
| bring | frog | goat | guess | laugh |
| bug | game | gold | guide | orange |
| egg | gap | grass | gum | right |
| enough | ghost | great | guy | strong |